Need for Speed

# Sprint Cars

by Bizzy Harris

Bullfrog Books

# Ideas for Parents and Teachers

Bullfrog Books let children practice reading informational text at the earliest reading levels. Repetition, familiar words, and photo labels support early readers.

## Before Reading

- Discuss the cover photo. What does it tell them?

- Look at the picture glossary together. Read and discuss the words.

## Read the Book

- "Walk" through the book and look at the photos. Let the child ask questions. Point out the photo labels.

- Read the book to the child, or have him or her read independently.

## After Reading

- Prompt the child to think more. Ask: Driving sprint cars can be dangerous. Would you like to drive one? Why or why not?

Bullfrog Books are published by Jump!
5357 Penn Avenue South
Minneapolis, MN 55419
www.jumplibrary.com

Library of Congress Cataloging-in-Publication Data

Names: Harris, Bizzy, author.
Title: Sprint cars / by Bizzy Harris.
Description: Minneapolis, MN: Jump!, Inc., [2023]
Series: Need for speed | Includes index.
Audience: Ages 5–8
Identifiers: LCCN 2021045323 (print)
LCCN 2021045324 (ebook)
ISBN 9781636906812 (hardcover)
ISBN 9781636906829 (paperback)
ISBN 9781636906836 (ebook)
Subjects: LCSH: Sprint cars—Juvenile literature.
Classification: LCC TL236.27 .H37 2023 (print)
LCC TL236.27 (ebook) | DDC 629.228—dc23
LC record available at
https://lccn.loc.gov/2021045323
LC ebook record available at
https://lccn.loc.gov/2021045324

Editor: Eliza Leahy
Designer: Emma Bersie

Photo Credits: john j. klaiber jr/Shutterstock, cover, 1, 3, 16–17, 22; Cal Sport Media/Alamy, 4, 10–11, 14, 20–21, 23tr, 23br; Grindstone Media Group/Shutterstock, 5, 23bl; Icon Sportswire/AP Images, 6–7; Bruce Alan Bennett/Shutterstock, 8, 15, 23tl; Ljupco Smokovski/Shutterstock, 9; WorldFoto/Alamy, 12–13; Rick Rea/Dreamstime, 18–19; dilemmadesigns/Shutterstock, 24.

Printed in the United States of America at Corporate Graphics in North Mankato, Minnesota.

# Table of Contents

# Big Wings

These sprint cars will race.

They will race on a track.

It is made of dirt.

dirt track

The race starts.
Cars drive laps.

helmet ····▶

cockpit
···
▼

Drivers sit in cockpits.
They wear helmets.

jumpsuit

## They wear jumpsuits, too.

wing

wing

This car has two big wings.
They keep the car stable.

# But cars can still crash.

A roll cage is made of strong bars.

roll cage

This car flips.

The cage hits the track.

The driver is safe.

This is a midget sprint car.

It is small.

It doesn't have wings.

This is an outlaw kart.
It makes a sharp turn!

Sprint car tires have good grip.

They help the cars turn quickly.

*Zoom!*

tire

# Parts of a Sprint Car

A sprint car can go 140 miles (225 kilometers) per hour. Take a look at its parts!

rear wing

front wing

roll cage

cockpit

engine

tire

# Picture Glossary

**flips**
Turns over quickly.

**grip**
To keep a tight hold
on something.

**laps**
Complete trips around
something, such as a track.

**stable**
Steady and not easily moved.

# Index

# To Learn More

**FACT SURFER**

**Finding more information is as easy as 1, 2, 3.**

❶ Go to www.factsurfer.com

❷ Enter "sprintcars" into the search box.

❸ Choose your book to see a list of websites.